HURRICANE DISASTER

LYNDA JONES

SCHOLASTIC INC.

NEW YORK | TORONTO | LONDON | AUCKLAND
SYDNEY | MEXICO CITY | NEW DELHI | HONG KONG

This book is dedicated to disaster victims and their loved ones, and to the scores
of selfless individuals who help survivors put their lives back together, piece by piece.
—L.J.

Designed by Mojo Media: Creative Director: Joe Funk; Art Director: Daniel Tideman

On Cover: Stocktrek Images/Getty, AP Photo/Matt Slocum, Dreamstime.com; page 1: NASA; page 2: Getty
Images; page 4: Dreamstime.com, AP Photo/Matt Slocum; page 5: AP Photo/Andy Newman; page 6: Dreamstime.
com, AP Photo/Charles Beeker; page 7: Dreamstime.com; page 8: Dreamstime.com; page 10: Dreamstime.
com; page 11: Courtesy of NASA; page 12: Charlie Bernatowicz; page 13: Courtesy of NASA; page 14: AP Photo/
Alan Diaz, Dreamstime.com, Courtesy of NASA; page 16: Getty Images/U.S. Coast Guard, Dreamstime.com,
Courtesy of NASA; page 17: Courtesy of NOAA; page 18: U.S. Air Force/Don Peek; page 19: Courtesy of U.S.
Air Force; page 20: AP Photo/Vincent Laforet; page 21: AP Photo/Eric Gay; page 22: Getty Images, AP Photo/
Sisters of Charity of the Incarnate Word; page 23: AFP/Getty Images, Time & Life Pictures/Getty Images, AP
Photo/Vincent Laforet; page 24: AP Photo/Smiley N. Pool, AP Photo/Andrea Booher, AP Photo/FEMA, Andrea
Booher; page 25: Courtesy of Deltec Homes, Dreamstime.com, AP Photo/Gerry Broome; page 26: Courtesy of
NASA; page 28: Stocktrek Images/Getty, Courtesy of U.S. Air Force; page 29: AP Photo/Nati Harnik, AP Photo/
Marta Lavandier; page 30: Courtesy of NASA, AP Photo/Gerry Broome; page 31: Dreamstime.com; page 31:
Courtesy of NASA, Dreamstime.com.

ISBN 978-0-545-34539-2

12 11 10 9 8 7 6 5 4 3 2 1   11 12 13 14 15 16/0

Printed in the U.S.A.   40
First printing, October 2011

**VIEW
FROM
THE TOP**

This is what a
hurricane looks like
from space.

CONTENTS

Alert! Alert!

A violent hurricane is pounding at sea and it's whirling toward land. Where will it strike?

Families gather in living rooms, eyes glued to the TV. They anxiously follow reports on the storm's progress. The National Hurricane Center issues a warning: The storm is getting stronger. It is expected to hit several U.S. states.

This hurricane could bring heavy rain and life-threatening winds. The public is in danger. City officials warn people to prepare for the storm. Citizens stock up on canned goods and bottled water. Homeowners board up their windows. Meanwhile, hundreds of shelters are opened as schools and businesses are shut down.

HURRICANE WARNING

EVACUA
ROUT

TFT LCD DIGITAL COLOR MONITOR/TV

THE TRUTH ABOUT HURRICANES

As scary as this scenario sounds, it is not unusual. Several hurricanes hit the U.S. each year. These forceful, spinning weather systems bring winds that move faster than 74 miles (119 kilometers) per hour.

When a hurricane strikes, it can unleash a steady downpour that lasts for days. Whipping winds can cause severe damage to everything in its path. Fruit and vegetable crops can be destroyed. Roads and homes can become flooded. The floods can wash away cars and bridges. Buildings can collapse. Power lines can topple. People can be harmed.

What can you do to survive a hurricane's furor? It helps to know when these ferocious storms occur and why.

HURRICANE HEADQUARTERS

Former National Hurricane Center Director Max Mayfield takes part in a news conference in 2006. The Center, located in Miami, Florida, is responsible for studying weather patterns and predicting the likelihood of hurricanes that could affect the U.S. and its territories. It updates the public on a storm's behavior.

Sea Monsters

Hurricanes are natural disasters. Humans have always feared their damaging powers. The word "hurricane," in fact, can be traced back to many different ancient civilizations.

ANCIENT RELICS The Mayas built grand pyramids (left) to worship their gods. The Taino's written language was in the form of carved symbols (right).

The Mayas (1800 BC to 900 AD) of Central America called their storm god "Hurakan." The Mayas believed that this god whipped up powerful and destructive storms whenever their actions angered him.

The Taino people, who began living in the Caribbean more than a thousand years ago, had a similar belief. They thought an evil god named "Huracan" unleashed the monstrous storms. Today, we know that science, not superstition, controls nature.

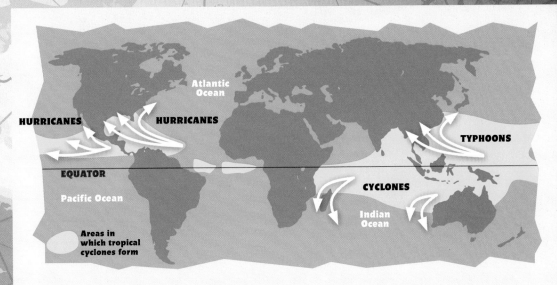

Atlantic Ocean

HURRICANES

HURRICANES

TYPHOONS

EQUATOR

Pacific Ocean

CYCLONES

Indian Ocean

Areas in which tropical cyclones form

A hurricane is actually a type of storm system called a tropical cyclone. Every year, about 90 of these storms strike around the world. In North, South, and Central America, they're called hurricanes. In regions near the western Pacific Ocean, people call them typhoons. They are known as cyclones in areas near the Indian Ocean.

Despite having different names, all tropical cyclones are almost exactly the same. These systems of thunderstorms form over warm seawater in the tropics and move in a spinning pattern. They can also strengthen or weaken as they travel thousands of miles across bodies of water.

As for differences: Tropical cyclones spin counterclockwise in the Northern Hemisphere and clockwise in the Southern Hemisphere. These storms also develop at different times of the year.

East Asian typhoons are most likely to form from June through December. In North and Central America, hurricanes can occur during the summer and early fall. For regions near the Atlantic Ocean, hurricane season spans from June 1 to November 30. By the Pacific Ocean, the season lasts from May 15 to November 30.

Did You Know? THE TERM **"cyclone"** COMES FROM GREEK WORDS MEANING COILS.

AIR FORCE

Winds from a hurricane can crumple buildings or even blow a car through the air like a toy. But winds, in general, are not always violent. They can be as light as a breeze. What is wind anyway, and how does it form?

You might not feel it, but there are 14.7 pounds of force pushing down on each square inch of your body. What's weighing you down? Air pressure.

Air is made of tiny particles called air molecules. Air also has weight. Air pressure is the weight of air pushing down on Earth. But air pressure changes from time to time. It is these changes that cause wind.

HOW WIND FORMS

1 Cold air is made of tightly packed air molecules. Warm air molecules, however, are more scattered. This makes cold air denser than warm air. Since warm air is lighter than cold air, it has lower pressure than cold air.

2 As a result, warm air rises. At the same time, heavier cold air sinks to replace the spot left by rising warm air. This continuous exchange of air creates wind. Basically, wind is moving air.

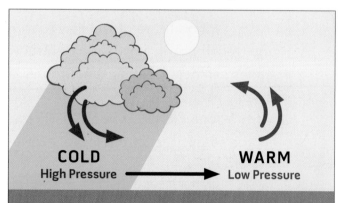

COLD
High Pressure ➡ WARM
Low Pressure

MIGHTY WIND

Winds can range from gentle to forceful. What is one way to estimate and describe their strengths? There is a system called the **Beaufort Wind Scale**.

Beaufort Number	Wind Speed		Description	Appearance of Wind Effects	
	MILES PER HOUR	KILOMETERS PER HOUR		ON LAND	ON WATER
0	Less than 1	Less than 1	Calm	Smoke rises straight up	Smooth as a mirror
1	1–3	1–5	Light air	Smoke drift indicates wind direction; still wind vanes	Slight ripples
2	4–7	6–11	Light breeze	Wind felt on face; leaves rustle	Small, short wavelets
3	8–12	12–19	Gentle breeze	Leaves and twigs in constant motion	Large wavelets, breaking crests
4	13–18	20–29	Moderate breeze	Small branches move	Small waves, many whitecaps
5	19–24	30–39	Fresh breeze	Small trees sway	Moderate waves, many whitecaps
6	25–31	40–50	Strong breeze	Large branches sway	Large waves, whitecaps, and spray
7	32–38	51–61	Near gale	Whole trees sway	Sea heaps up, white foam blows
8	39–46	62–74	Gale	Twigs break off trees	Moderately high, long waves, well marked off by sea foam
9	47–54	75–87	Strong gale	Branches break off trees; slight structural damage	High waves, rolling seas, dense foam
10	55–63	88–102	Storm	Trees uprooted; major property damage	Large waves with overhanging crests, sea white with foam
11	64–73	103–118	Violent storm	Severe property damage	Waves over 30 feet (9 meters), limited visibility
12	74 or more	119 or more	Hurricane	Houses and land destroyed	Waves over 45 feet (13.7 meters), minimal visibility

Hurricanes do not form just anywhere. They all begin life over warm tropical waters. You'll find these waters just north or south of the equator. Under the right conditions, a storm in this region can grow through four stages and turn into a full-blown hurricane.

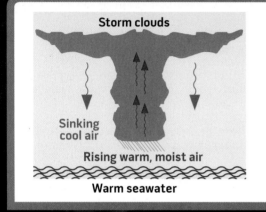

Storm clouds

Sinking cool air

Rising warm, moist air

Warm seawater

STAGE 1: TROPICAL DISTURBANCE

In the tropics, the sun can heat seawater to more than 80°F (27°C). This high temperature causes water to quickly evaporate into the air. As this warm, moist air rises, cooler air rushes in to take its place. This air, too, quickly becomes warm and rises. As the moist air travels upward, it cools and condenses into storm clouds. Result: thunderstorms with winds measuring less than 23 miles (37 kilometers) per hour.

STAGE 2: TROPICAL DEPRESSION

Warm seawater continues to build thunderstorms. Many storms cluster together. Winds strengthen and begin to blow in a circle. A rotating column of air begins to form in the center of the storm system. Winds range from 23 to 38 miles (37 to 61 kimometers) per hour.

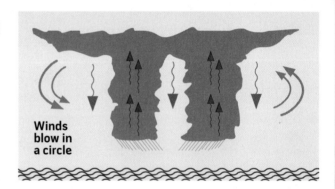

Winds blow in a circle

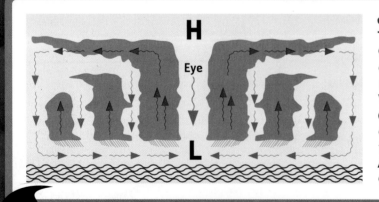

H

Eye

L

STAGE 3: TROPICAL STORM

Cooler, high pressure areas (H) continue to push into warmer, low pressure areas (L). The storm grows. Winds intensify, reaching 39 to 73 miles (63 to 117 kimometers) per hour. A well-defined column of air, called the eye, forms at the center of the storm system. At this stage, the National Hurricane Center gives the storm a name.

STAGE 4: TROPICAL CYCLONE

The storm becomes severe. When the winds exceed 74 miles (119 kilometers) per hour, the storm is officially called a hurricane. This image shows Hurricane Rita, which plowed into many southern states in September 2005. It brought winds that blew as fast as 180 miles (285 kilometers) per hour.

If you're stuck in the middle of a hurricane, you would see endless downpour and wind-whipped objects. But if you could travel to space and look down from above, you'd see a very different picture.

From above, a hurricane resembles a jumbo donut. All hurricanes have a round, spiraling shape with an opening in the middle. A typical hurricane can measure approximately 300 miles (480 kilometers) wide and up to 50,000 feet (15 kilometers) high. Let's zoom in on this picture.

EYE This is the center of the hurricane. This tube-shaped column measures between 20 to 40 miles (32 to 64 kimometers) wide. It spans all the way from the top of the storm to the sea. Cool, sinking air (blue arrows) prevents cloud formation and rain. Believe it or not, it is relatively clear and calm here.

WIND DIRECTION Hurricanes in the Northern Hemisphere blow counterclockwise. This spinning motion, caused by Earth's rotation, is called the Coriolis effect. The winds spiral toward the eye, gaining speed as they move inward. But at high altitudes, the winds weaken. They spiral clockwise out through the storm cap (purple arrows at the top).

HURRICANE

EYEWALL This part surrounds the eye of the storm. Unlike the eye, this part is far from calm. It is a dense ring of tall thunderstorms. These storms produce the heaviest rain and the strongest, fastest winds in the entire system. Some can blow up to 180 miles (290 kilometers) per hour.

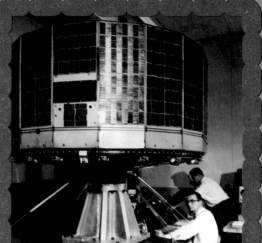

DID YOU KNOW?

In 1961, NASA's TIROS-3 satellite transmitted to Earth some of the earliest images of hurricanes ever captured from space.

SPIRAL RAINBANDS These spiral curved bands of thunderstorm clouds can extend hundreds of miles from the eye of the hurricane. They bring rain, lightning, and, sometimes, tornadoes. Often, there are gaps in between the bands. It doesn't rain in those spots.

Blow, Wind, Blow

Hurricanes don't happen overnight.

They can take days or even weeks to develop. Spinning winds inside a hurricane, along with weather systems outside, can drive a cyclone to travel thousands of miles across the sea. As it travels, it can change path. A hurricane can also gain or lose strength, depending on if there's a steady supply of warm water to feed the storm.

Why Do Hurricanes Have Names?

Before 1950, meteorologists named storms after their location and date. This system was confusing because more than one hurricane can form at any one time. In 1953, the National Hurricane Center began creating a list of women's names to use for naming Atlantic hurricanes. Today, the list consists of 21 alternating men's and women's names in alphabetical order. The names are repeated every six years. If a certain named storm is particularly damaging, the name is retired and another one replaces it.

The Saffir-Simpson Hurricane Wind Scale

In 1971, scientists Herbert Saffir and Robert Simpson developed a scale that ranks the intensity of hurricanes from 1 to 5. A Category 1 hurricane is weakest and a Category 5 storm is strongest. The scale has gone through many changes throughout the years. The version updated in 2010 categorizes a hurricane according to its wind speeds. It also describes the potential damage caused by the winds.

CATEGORY DAMAGE	WIND SPEEDS	EXAMPLES
1 Very dangerous winds will produce some damage	**74-95** Miles Per Hour **119-153** Kilometers Per Hour	▶ Roof shingles can fly off. Unanchored motor homes can shift or roll off foundations. ▶ Windows may break if struck by debris. ▶ Masonry chimneys can topple. ▶ Large branches of trees can snap. ▶ Damage to power lines can cause power outages that could last for days.
2 Extremely dangerous winds will cause extensive damage	**96-110** Miles Per Hour **154-177** Kilometers Per Hour	▶ Significant damage to mobile homes. Well-constructed frame homes could experience major roof and siding damage. ▶ Shallowly rooted trees can topple, blocking roads. ▶ Widespread power loss expected. Outages could last from days to weeks.
3 Devastating damage will occur	**111-130** Miles Per Hour **178-209** Kilometers Per Hour	▶ Roofs can blow off of frame homes. Exterior walls of mobile homes can crumble. ▶ Most commercial signs destroyed. ▶ Electricity can be unavailable for several days to a few weeks after the storm passes.
4 Catastrophic damage will occur	**131-155** Miles Per Hour **210-249** Kilometers Per Hour	▶ Walls of poorly constructed homes can collapse. ▶ Most windows will be blown out of high-rise buildings. ▶ Most trees and power poles downed. ▶ Power outages can last for weeks to possibly months.
5 Catastrophic damage will occur	**155+** Miles Per Hour **249+** Kilometers Per Hour	▶ A high percentage of wood homes destroyed. Possible complete collapse of buildings. ▶ Nearly all trees uprooted and power poles downed. Power outages can last for possibly months. Affected areas can be uninhabitable for weeks or months.

Where's the Storm?

You may have seen meteorologists on TV reporting on a hurricane's development. They often show a map that pinpoints the location of the storm. The map usually includes a path showing where the hurricane is expected to move. How do meteorologists predict a cyclone's route? They rely on a variety of weather instruments for help. Here are some:

SURFACE OBSERVATIONS Some ships and special buoys placed all over the ocean carry weather instruments. They measure air and water temperatures, air pressure, and wave conditions. They then transmit the information to scientists on land.

Scientists enter the collected data into weather-forecasting computers. These computers make billions of mathematical calculations to create a model of a storm. Weather forecasters analyze this information to make their own determination about where a hurricane will hit.

DOPPLER RADAR This device measures the direction and speed of moving things. It zeros in on raindrops, determining if they are moving toward or away from the radar. Through this information, scientists can estimate the intensity of rain, as well as wind direction and speed.

WEATHER SATELLITES These unmanned spacecraft circle Earth. Some hover about 23,000 miles (37,000 kilometers) above ground. Each satellite usually has two main types of instruments. One type scans Earth to create visual pictures of cloud patterns. During the nighttime, clouds are hard to see. So another type of instrument detects energy from clouds. By mapping out the differences in energy, scientists can "see" cloud movement even in the dark.

SAT AM

FRI AM

THUR AM

WED AM

TUES AM

85 MPH

125 MPH

40 MPH

45 MPH

Meet a Hurricane Tracker

NAME: **DR. RICHARD PASCH**

JOB: **SENIOR HURRICANE SPECIALIST, THE NATIONAL HURRICANE CENTER**

What do you do?

The National Hurricane Center is responsible for tracking and predicting tropical cyclones over an area that includes the Atlantic basin, north of the equator, and the eastern North Pacific Ocean. I analyze data to forecast where a hurricane may strike.

What's the most challenging thing about your job?

I'd say predicting rapid changes in a hurricane's intensity. Computer models that simulate the circulation and motion of a hurricane are very successful at predicting its future track. But those same models don't simulate the changes in a hurricane's strengths very well.

Are there ways to improve forecasting intensity?

One of the main efforts underway is the Hurricane Forecast Improvement Project. Over the next ten years, our goal is to be able to predict rapid intensity change and also improve forecasts of hurricane intensity by 50 percent.

How does your work help the public?

We try to keep people informed about hurricane threats. We want to allow them to have enough time to take caution should one hit. We try to be realistic about the level of threat, but we do have to have some precautions to allow for the uncertainty of our forecast.

HURRICANE HUNTERS

How close can we really get to a hurricane?
For some people, it's their job to brave pounding rain, lightning, and a really bumpy ride to get right into the middle of one. The National Hurricane Center relies on special aircraft that fly right into the eye of a swirling storm to collect data. Meet the Hurricane Hunters.

THE PLANE
The Hurricane Hunters use a tough, four-engine plane to fly into tropical cyclones. The plane is outfitted with a variety of weather-measuring instruments. It's like a flying laboratory. Onboard instruments include:

The dropsonde is dropped from a chute on board the plane into the eyewall of the hurricane. As the instrument parachutes all the way down to the ocean, it transmits data about air temperature, wind speed and direction, and atmospheric pressure.

The stepped frequency microwave radiometer measures surface wind and rain rate on the ocean's surface every second.

The dew point hygrometer measures the amount of moisture in the atmosphere.

The anemometer measures wind speed.

U.S. AIR FORCE

Meet a Crew Member

NAME: CAPTAIN DOUGLAS GAUTRAU

JOB: AERIAL RECONNAISSANCE WEATHER OFFICER OF THE HURRICANE HUNTERS

WHAT DO YOU DO? I'm the onboard meteorologist and I act as the mission director. I tell the crew where we need to fly and where we're going to release our weather instruments.

HOW MANY TIMES DO YOU FLY THROUGH THE EYE OF ONE STORM? About four or five times. We go through the northwest, northeast, southwest, and southeast quadrants of the eye constantly.

WHAT'S THE WORST STORM YOU'VE EVER ENCOUNTERED UP CLOSE? I've flown about 50 storm missions over the last four years. The worst was Hurricane Paula in 2010. It was a Category 1 storm that wasn't stacked vertically like a normal storm; it was slanted. We caught a lot of turbulence, which made it a very bumpy ride.

WHY DON'T THE STRONG WINDS BLOW YOUR PLANE AWAY? When we get into the eyewall of a major hurricane, we have to turn the aircraft slightly to the left into the wind. We call that crabbing. If you fly straight toward the eye and you have a crosswind on your left, you're going to be blown to the right. You're going to miss the eye. So you go in sideways.

HOW DOES YOUR DATA HELP FORECASTERS AND THE PUBLIC? With each mission, we send data to the National Hurricane Center every ten minutes. It helps the meteorologists improve their forecast of the hurricanes strength and movement by 25 percent.

The crew consists of members of the Air Force Reserve's 53rd Weather Reconnaissance Squadron. There is a pilot, co-pilot, and a navigator. There's also a loadmaster, who releases the dropsonde into the hurricane. In addition, there's an aerial reconnaissance weather officer. Let's meet him.

INST

UNDER WATER

News of a brewing hurricane can cause people to bite their nails with anticipation. Perhaps the most anxious are those who live near coastal regions. These areas are in the front line of a barreling storm. A direct hit can cause severe damage and harm many lives.

Hurricanes can knock down buildings and uproot trees. Pelting winds can also kill crops and harm animals. But did you know that some of the worst hurricane disasters involve water? **Drowning is the cause of more than 90 percent of hurricane deaths.**

STORM SURGE

For coastal regions, one of the greatest threats from a hurricane is a storm surge. This is a sudden rise in sea level.

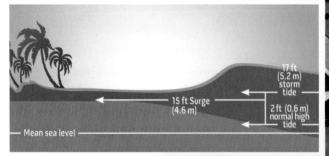

17 ft (5.2 m) storm tide

15 ft Surge (4.6 m)

2 ft (0.6 m) normal high tide

Mean sea level

As a hurricane travels, winds above the ocean's surface push water toward the eye of the hurricane. As the storm moves toward land and travels up the coastline, this water bulge mounds up.

Then, *whoosh.* The mound unleashes. A wall of water more than 15 feet (4.6 meters) tall crashes ashore. It can crush homes and cause major flooding. What's even more severe than a storm surge? Storm tide. That's when a storm surge occurs during high tides.

Hurricane Katrina slammed into New Orleans, LA, on August 29, 2005. As much as 80 percent of the city became flooded.

FLOODING

Besides storm surges, torrential downpour from a hurricane can also flood roads and entire towns. Heavy rain can also create dangerous mudslides. When hilly regions become saturated with water, the soil liquefies. As the mud accelerates downhill, it carries with it large items, like cars, trees, and boulders.

MUDSLIDE This car was buried by a mudslide caused by Hurricane Ike. The storm tore through the Caribbean and many U.S. states in September 2008.

DID YOU KNOW?

A hurricane can produce tornadoes. A tornado, which is a rotating, funnel-shaped column of air, can suck up everything in its path. Nearly all of the hurricanes that make landfall in the U.S. spawn tornadoes. In 2004, Hurricane Ivan whipped up a record-breaking 117 tornadoes across the U.S. as it traveled toward land.

HISTORIC HURRICANES

HOW CATASTROPHIC CAN A HURRICANE GET?
HERE ARE SOME OF THE WORST CYCLONES EVER RECORDED.

GALVESTON HURRICANE OF 1900

AREA AFFECTED: **GALVESTON, TEXAS**
DATE: **SEPTEMBER 8, 1900**
STRENGTH: **CATEGORY 4**
CASUALTIES: **BETWEEN 6,000 AND 12,000**

At the turn of the twentieth century, Galveston was a popular city island with a population of 38,000. On September 5, weather forecasters predicted that a hurricane was heading from Cuba toward Florida and other East Coast regions. But the storm changed direction, hitting Galveston instead. Citizens had no time to evacuate. The storm surge's gigantic waves sucked people into the sea and buried the entire town underwater.

RECORD: Deadliest Hurricane in U.S. History

HURRICANE KATRINA

AREA AFFECTED: COASTAL REGIONS OF LOUISIANA, MISSISSIPPI, AND ALABAMA   DATE: **AUGUST 29, 2005**   STRENGTH: **CATEGORY 5**
CASUALTIES: **1,836 DEAD; 705 MISSING**

Hurricane Katrina slammed into the Gulf Coast. Heavy rains and 140 miles (225 kilometers) per hour winds tore through the region. New Orleans, a city in Louisiana, was one of the hardest hit. The city sits below sea level and relies on a system of pumps and wall-like barriers, or levees, to prevent flooding. The system failed. A storm surge as high as 30 feet (9 meters) crashed through the levees; 80 percent of the city lay underwater. Katrina caused about $75 billion in damages.

RECORD: Costliest Natural Disaster in U.S. History

GREAT BHOLA CYCLONE

AREA AFFECTED: BANGLADESH   DATE: **NOVEMBER 12-13, 1970**
STRENGTH: **CATEGORY 3**   CASUALTIES: **BETWEEN 300,000 AND 500,000**

Poor farming and fishing families weren't readily equipped with phones or TV sets. So most didn't get news that they were in the path of a cyclone churning in the Bay of Bengal—an arm of the Indian Ocean. During the night, the people were awakened by winds howling at 140 miles (225 kilometers) per hour. Storm surge rushed ashore. Catastrophic flooding and winds destroyed complete villages. Nearly 46,000 of the region's estimated 77,000 fishermen died. Approximately 65 percent of the coastal region's fishing industry was destroyed.

RECORD: Deadliest Cyclone Ever Recorded

HURRICANE MITCH

AREA AFFECTED: HONDURAS, NICARAGUA, GUATEMALA, AND EL SALVADOR   DATE: **OCTOBER 29 TO NOVEMBER 4, 1998**
STRENGTH: **CATEGORY 1**   CASUALTIES: **11,000 DEAD; THOUSANDS MISSING**

Slow-moving Mitch made landfall in Honduras on October 29, 1998. Although the winds weakened, heavy rains continued nonstop for days as the storm moved at a snail's pace across Central America. The torrential rain caused massive flooding. Floods washed away bridges, roads, and towns. Mountainous regions became saturated with water. Tons of mud barreled down hills, burying families alive in their homes. Mudslides and floods left more than three million people homeless.

RECORD: Deadliest Hurricane to Hit Central America

RESCUE
MISSION

Once a hurricane hits land, it gradually dies out. That's because it no longer has warm seawater to stoke its growth. Even if a hurricane is long gone, its messy aftermath can be lasting.

Right after a severe storm, disaster-relief workers race to the scene to help those in need. For this reason, they are called first responders. Learn how they provide aid.

SHELTER Hurricanes can severely damage homes, leaving families without a place to live. Organizations like the Red Cross send volunteers to set up temporary shelters. After Hurricane Katrina in 2005, the Red Cross housed more than 5,000 people in 26 shelters in New Orleans. In 2008, the organization served more than six million meals to hurricane survivors.

WATER A hurricane can have devastating effects on water supply. How? When floods happen, it can cause raw sewage—human waste, food scraps, and other waste—to flow into wells and other water supply systems. Drinking contaminated water can cause diseases, such as cholera, that may result in severe illness or death.

The Federal Emergency Management Agency sends truckloads of ice and bottled water to a disaster area. Each of these trucks can supply enough water for 5,000 people. The agency also has tanker trucks. Each one can provide 6,500 gallons (24,600 liters) of water for cooking and bathing.

CLEANUP Downed trees, building debris, and other damages can harm humans and the environment. Often, the U.S. Army Corp of Engineers rushes in to organize cleanup efforts. The Corps is also responsible for rebuilding roads, bridges, floodwalls, and other structures that have been damaged or destroyed.

Meet a Home Rebuilding Expert

NAME: **STEVE LINTON**

JOB: **DIRECTOR OF SUSTAINABLE TECHNOLOGIES FOR DELTEC HOMES**

What do you do? I help customers build homes that can withstand extreme environments. After Hurricane Katrina in 2005, I worked with a team to rebuild severely damaged homes in Louisiana.

The homes you design are round. Why? The round shape has unique advantages. When winds hit the long wall of a rectangular home, pressure can build up. This pressure can damage parts of the house or even blow it over. With a round home, there aren't any long sections for that pressure to build up. The air, instead, flows around the home, making the home more durable.

What else makes these homes sturdy? The roof and floor systems are made of trusses. These trusses gather in the center and resemble the spokes on the wheel of a bike. Believe it or not, bike wheels are very strong. If there's heavy wind coming from one angle, the roof system can distribute the pressure from the wind throughout the entire house. That way, no one spot will take on the wind's full impact.

TALLY UP ↗

HURRICANE KATRINA

Some hurricane seasons are stronger than others.

For a long time, the average number of Atlantic Ocean–spawned tropical storms was ten a year. Six of which became hurricanes. Since the mid-1990s, the average jumped to 15 tropical storms a year, with eight blowing up into hurricanes. Scientists have been puzzling over why hurricanes in the Atlantic are becoming more frequent.

┌ 2005 ┐

27 NAMED STORMS **14** HURRICANES

FOUR CATEGORY 5 STORMS: (EMILY, KATRINA, RITA, AND WILMA)

Storm Year
2005 and 2010 tied for the warmest year in over a century. A record-breaking number of tropical storms and hurricanes brewed over the Atlantic Ocean. Because of the large number of tropical storms, the National Hurricane Center used up all the names on its annual storm-naming list. After the last name was used, the center named the subsequent storms after the Greek alphabet: Alpha, Beta, Gamma, Delta, Epsilon, and Zeta.

Aug 27 2005

ONE POSSIBILITY

Some scientists believe that global warming may be the cause. Scientists agree that Earth has warmed about 1.8°F (1°C) in the last 100 years. They don't, however, agree on why or how. Some scientists believe that humans are behind Earth's rising temperature. When humans burn fossil fuels, carbon dioxide gas is released into the atmosphere. This gas traps heat over Earth, causing the planet and its oceans to warm. Warmer oceans may produce larger and more intense hurricanes.

ANOTHER POSSIBILITY

Other scientists believe that the warming of Earth and the change in climate may be normal. They think the increase in Earth's temperature is due to a natural shift in warm ocean currents that occurs every 20 to 30 years.

During this 20- to 30-year cycle, there are more frequent storms. This warm period is followed by 20 to 30 years of cooler water, and, therefore, fewer hurricanes.

THE BOTTOM LINE ▼

No one is certain for now. Whatever the reason, a warm Earth can cause hurricanes.

Hot Water

Water temperatures in the Atlantic Ocean are warmest during September. Most hurricanes occur during this month.

Typical Hurricane Frequency by Month

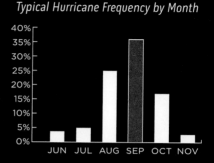

Typical Tropical Storm Formation Zones

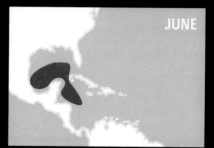

JUNE

SEPTEMBER

NOVEMBER

HOW TO STOP A HURRICANE

Some scientists believe that hurricanes are too massive and powerful to squash.

But some think otherwise.
Here are some innovative ideas
from past and present.

PROJECT STORMFURY Between 1962 and 1983, the U.S. government experimented with controlling hurricanes. A plane would fly over a storm and spray the chemical silver iodide into its clouds. This method, called cloud seeding, encourages ice crystals to grow. This, in turn, encourages rain. Scientists thought that this procedure would disrupt the natural hurricane-building process. After years of research, they concluded that this method didn't reduce a hurricane's strength. The project was abandoned.

Pictured left is the 1966 crew of Project Stormfury.

COLD WATER TREATMENT

Microsoft founder Bill Gates (pictured near left) and a team of inventors at Intellectual Ventures think they've found a way that can disrupt hurricanes before they make landfall. Their idea: have barges equipped with water pumps pull cold water from the bottom of the ocean to the surface. Without warm surface water, hurricanes can't form. The inventors are still doing research. It's uncertain if this idea could be successfully put into practice.

POWDER POWER

Dyn-O-Gel is a powder that absorbs moisture, converting it into a gel. Florida businessman Peter Cordani (pictured right) developed the chemical in the 1990s. He thinks dumping large quantities of the substance from an aircraft into the clouds of a hurricane would help slow the storm.

His belief: The powder absorbs rain droplets, converting them into tiny flakelike gel particles. Hurricanes need warm, moist air to stay alive. If the gel reduces the moisture in the air, the storm's intensity would reduce.

Cordani believes his product will not harm the public or the environment. When the gel falls into the ocean, it dissolves. Over land, most of the gel evaporates into the air.

Although the inventor has tested Dyn-O-Gel over storm clouds in Florida, it's not ready to fight hurricanes. He hopes to raise more funds for research and eventually sell his product to the U.S. government.

Future Forecast

Although scientists have not found a way to prevent hurricanes, they are researching ways to better predict storm paths and intensity. They hope their findings can lead to better ways to protect the public.

For now, what's the best way to survive the punch of a raging hurricane? By being prepared and informed.

WEATHERING THE STORM

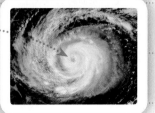

When the National Hurricane Center knows that a progressing storm can bring real threats, they warn people to take precautions. They raise these two types of alerts:

Single Flag

Hurricane Watch:
This alerts that hurricane conditions are possible within a specified coastal area. It is issued 48 hours before the anticipated arrival of tropical-storm-force winds.

Double Flag

Hurricane Warning:
This warns that hurricane conditions are expected somewhere within a specified coastal area. This warning is issued 36 hours before the anticipated arrival of tropical-storm-force winds.

These flags alert boaters of threat level.

COUNTDOWN CHECKLIST

If your area is hurricane-prone, the best thing for you and your family to have is an emergency plan lined up in advance. Here are some basic things that you should do or have on hand during each level of emergency.

Level: Hurricane Watch

☑ Have a **battery-operated or crank radio** on hand for updates on the storm's progress.

☑ Stock up on **first-aid supplies**, **canned foods**, **batteries**, and **drinking water**.

☑ **Designate a meeting place** in your neighborhood for family members.

☑ Put together a **disaster kit** filled with a flashlight, a change of clothes, sturdy shoes, and bedding.

Level: Hurricane Warning

☑ **Be prepared to evacuate immediately.**

☑ **Have a plan for where your pets can stay** if you can't take them with you.

☑ Have the **phone numbers** of family members on hand.

Glossary

Air pressure: Weight of air pushing down on Earth

Condense: To change from a gas or vapor into a liquid

Equator: Imaginary line that circles Earth midway between the South Pole and North Pole

Evacuate: To leave an area under threat, moving to a safer location

Evaporate: To change from a liquid into a gas or vapor

Global warming: An increase in the average temperature of Earth's oceans and atmosphere

Hurricane: A spinning weather system that brings winds that move faster than 74 miles (119 kilometers) per hour

Meteorologist: A scientist who specializes in studying weather

Molecules: Neutral group of two or more atoms. An atom is the smallest possible particle of a chemical element.

Radar: Device that uses radio to pinpoint the location of objects

Saturate: To soak completely

Storm surge: A sudden rise in sea level caused by winds pushing toward seawater toward coast

Storm tide: Storm surge that occurs during high tides

Tropics: Areas on Earth that lie about 1,600 miles (2,600 kilometers) north and south of the equator

Weather satellite: An unmanned spacecraft that orbits Earth, recording information about weather